Stefan

1983

To Stefan

Love,
Helen +
Lee

Summer
1983

The Color Nature Library

CATS

By
PEGGY WRATTEN

Designed by
DAVID GIBBON

Produced by
TED SMART

CRESCENT BOOKS

First published in Great Britain 1977 by
Colour Library International Ltd.

Designed by David Gibbon.
Produced by Ted Smart.
© Text: Peggy Wratten.
© Illustrations: Colour Library International Ltd.

Colour separations by
La Cromolito, Milan, Italy.

Display and Text filmsetting by
Focus Photoset, London, England.

Printed in Spain by Grijelmo, S.A.

Published by Crescent Books, a division of
Crown Publishers Inc.

CRESCENT 1978

INTRODUCTION

For countless generations the cat and the dog have been man's companions. Man was able to train the dog to work for him and to obey him but the cat has always kept its independence, as epitomised in Rudyard Kipling's story *The cat that walked by itself*. This is because in the wild the cat is solitary, hunting on its own and able to fend for itself, pairing up for a short time only in the breeding season. The dog, on the other hand, is a social animal, living in packs in the wild, showing loyalty to a leader and having to conform to the rules of the pack. Even though the cat works for us by catching mice and rats it does so because it is by nature a hunter and not because man trained it for this.

So, in some respects, the cat has changed little from its wild ancestors. Although we still are not sure of its origin it is likely it was derived from the cafer or bush cat of Africa with perhaps a strain from the European wild cat. Both of these are tabby with narrow dark vertical stripes and a bushy ringed tail. The domestic striped tabby has similar striping but the domestic blotched tabby, the most common in the British Isles, has blotchy black markings and broad longitudinal stripes. The typical short-haired domestic cat is about 2½ feet long including a 9-inch tapering tail. The weight varies considerably but can reach 21 pounds.

The cat is thought to have been first domesticated by the Egyptians but even this is not certain and it is probable that small wild cats have been tamed by man to some degree since prehistoric times. In Ancient Egypt the cat was regarded as sacred and held in much reverence. There are many pictures of cats in Egyptian antiquities and mummified cats have been found in old Egyptian tombs. The Egyptians even had a cat goddess called Bast of Pasht. It has been suggested that 'puss' is derived from 'Bast' but it is more likely puss is an imitation of the cat's hiss.

Since the days of Ancient Egypt there have been all sorts of superstitions and legends about cats. In the Middle Ages in Britain it used to be thought that a black cat brought ill luck as it was supposed to be the witch's 'familiar' and the devil was sometimes portrayed as a black cat. In view of this it is strange that in the 17th and 18th centuries the body of a cat and a rat were often put into a cavity in the wall of a new house in England, some say to keep out the devil, others say to keep out the rats. Today a black cat is supposed to be lucky and many people are pleased to see a black cat cross their path. However, it is a different story in most other parts of the world where the black cat is still thought to be unlucky and a white cat is thought to be lucky.

Whatever its origin and whatever the superstitions about it the cat is a familiar and much loved member of many households today all over the world. Although the most usual colour is tabby there are many colour varieties: black, white, ginger, marmalade, tortoiseshell, silver, even blue. There are now many different breeds of cats, not all recognised in every country. America especially has been very active in introducing many new varieties. There are basically two groups: short-haired and long-haired. The short-haired contain such exotic varieties as the Siamese and the Abyssinian and also the tailless Manx; the long-haired include the Persian, the Angora and the Black Long-hair. There is not enough space in this book to describe all the different breeds but there are many delightful colour photographs included to give some idea of all the many varieties. Suffice it to say that breeds like many other things come and go in fashions, and every cat owner probably thinks their cat is the most attractive and affectionate, even if it is only a backyard 'mog' or alley cat as it is called in America.

The cat is a hardy creature and if looked after well will live happily with you for many years. This book does not attempt to tell you how to look after your pet–there are many other excellent books telling you all about this–but it will tell you what your cat does, how it does it and why. It will tell you about its sight, its hearing and how it communicates. It will tell you about grooming sunbathing, playing and about the cat's intelligence. It will also tell you about some out-of-the-ordinary cats. In short this book will be about the cat's way of life.

Left, White longhair and Siamese-type shorthair kittens.

Previous page, Cream longhair kittens

Temperament

Perhaps of all domestic animals the cat is the one that manages to live with man and yet keep its independence. Its air of self-reliance has given rise to the idea that cats adopted man for their own advantage rather than having been domesticated by man. It is true that a cat likes to go its own way and sometimes seems to be more attached to a home than to its owner but this may depend on how it is treated. If a cat is looked after well and given as much freedom as possible it will settle down contentedly in any home. Indeed most domestic cats are very lovable creatures needing human companionship and affection.

An individual cat may become so attached to you that it will be waiting at the door for you on your return home. It will walk round and round your legs purring loudly and making a great fuss of you. Admittedly, the next minute it may see a bird in the garden and will have shot out of the door and seemingly forgotten all about you, but that is how a cat is. Affectionate one moment and off on its own business the next.

Left, Chinchilla.
Above and right, Bicoloured longhair.

Cats are comfort-loving animals. They will take endless trouble to find just the right place to snooze in on a sunny day and then stretch out luxuriantly in the sun. Or in the evening by the fire a cat will jump onto your lap, purring contentedly and invite you to stroke it behind the ears or under the chin.

So it is very evident that a cat likes to be made a fuss of so long as it chooses its own time for this. Being a dignified animal, however, it does not like to be teased. Although it is far more tolerant of children and will put up with a young child pulling it about and teasing it for a certain time, it will eventually lose patience and may even scratch.

A cat is a creature of habit and likes an ordered life with its food put out for it regularly, and most cats have very definite preferences for certain foods. Some cats show their affection more when about to be fed so that it has been suggested that a cat's affection has more than a hint of 'cupboard love'!

It is unfair to generalise too much about cats. Each one has its own character and personality. Some are more affectionate than others, some more intelligent, some more timid or placid. Different breeds and varieties have their own special characteristics. However loving a cat may be it should never be over-pampered. It is still basically a wild animal and its domestication is little more than skin-deep, as shown by the ease with which a cat can go back to the wild and become feral.

Looking around

It might be expected that an animal naturally nocturnal as the cat would use its senses of smell and hearing more than its sight. But this is not so. A cat's eyes can make the maximum use of all possible light at night. In dim light the muscles of the iris relax allowing the pupils to open wide so admitting as much light as possible. Behind the retina of the eye is a layer of silvery crystals called the tapetum which acts as a reflector. Much of the light which enters a normal eye passes through the retina and is lost, absorbed in the tissues behind it. The tapetum reflects such light back, so there is a second chance for it to strike the receptor cells in the retina. So no light is lost. When a cat is caught in the headlights of a car it is the rays from these lights reflected back from the tapetum that cause its eyes to glow.

Top left, White longhair.
Left, Black shorthair.
Right, Tabby shorthair.

So it is when hunting at night. The cat stalks its prey with infinite patience and stealth using its sight as well as its hearing to good effect.

During the day the muscles of the iris contract to make the pupils slitlike, so protecting the cat's eyes by excluding the bright rays of full daylight. In daylight also it has been found that a cat has faint colour vision.

Hearing

Although a cat's hearing is acute it is especially so for high-pitched sounds. This is probably why a cat responds more readily to a woman's voice. Like many other mammals a cat's hearing extends beyond the range of the human ear into the higher frequencies. When waiting beside a mousehole a cat is probably hearing the rodents' voices when these are inaudible to our ears.

A cat soon learns the particular sounds that affect it in any household: the sound of its tin of food being opened or its plate put on the ground, the sound of its owner's car coming into the drive or its own name being called. This last it will ignore quite blatantly if it does not want to come in at that particular moment!

Above and left, Seal-point Siamese.

Some years ago it was discovered that all-white cats with blue eyes are usually deaf. If one or two coloured hairs are present amongst the white, then the cat has normal hearing and equally if a white cat has only one blue eye. The reason why all-white cats with blue eyes are usually deaf is not fully understood but the lack of hearing does not seem to affect a cat's hunting powers or its relationships with other cats.

Smell and touch

All mammals have a sense of smell but in some it is more developed than in others. To illustrate this: inside the nose of mammals is a smelling membrane with many receptor cells. In our membrane there are only 5 million cells but in the best tracker dogs there are 220 million and each works more efficiently than ours. A cat's sense of smell is also very sensitive. It uses it for selecting food and together with its very acute sense of taste it knows immediately

Right, Seal-point Siamese.
Below, Blue-point Siamese.

what food it likes. A cat will go into ecstacies over the smell of catnip and will enjoy the scent of other garden flowers. But more importantly a cat, by smell, can recognise a long way off whether another cat is a male or female and a tom will avoid the territory of another tomcat that has been marked with its urine.

It has long been accepted that a cat's whiskers are organs of touch helping the cat to feel its way in the dark. Much in the same way as we would walk down an unlighted corridor at night with our hands held in front of us to feel for possible obstacles, so a cat's whiskers are brought forward reaching well in front of the face as soon as it starts to move.

Left, Blue-point and Tabby- or Lynx-point Siamese.
Below, Blue-point Siamese.
Right, Seal-point Siamese

Sleep and comfort

It has been estimated that cats spend up to two-thirds of their lives asleep! The cat seems to be the very symbol of comfort curled up in its basket or stretched out sunbathing in the garden. Perhaps because the domestic cat is descended from the African bush cat it always seeks out the warmest places to sleep. Research into cats' sleeping positions has shown that the position alters with the temperature of the surrounding air. At the lowest temperatures a cat curls up in a full circle, with the head and paws tucked together against the belly and the tail wrapped round them. As the temperature rises the cat gradually uncurls until it is finally stretched out at full-length.

Much the same thing can be noticed with a mother cat and her kittens. When first born the kittens are not capable of keeping themselves warm and are dependent on their mother for warmth. At first the mother cat spends most of her time curled round her kittens in the basket so they are always in contact with her body. When she leaves them the kittens huddle together for warmth. On a really hot day, however, the litter will be found lying as far apart as possible.

As well as the enjoyment that a cat gets from sleeping, nobody owning a cat can fail to notice the satisfaction it gets from washing and grooming itself. In washing itself the cat uses its tongue and its paws. The tongue is very rough, excellent for cleaning the fur. The front paws are wetted by the tongue and used to get to the places the cat cannot lick directly. The cat washes its face first, wiping its eyes, around the ears and its cheeks. The body is then washed all over, the legs being raised in turn to get to the more inaccessible places. Mother cats seem to be washing their kittens most of the time and from this the kittens soon learn to wash themselves.

The obvious enjoyment a cat feels on being stroked or petted suggests that grooming is at least in part a social activity. Most social animals groom each other to maintain social bonds and although a cat is naturally a solitary animal, social grooming would occur between mother and kitten and between the male and female in the breeding period.

Far left, top, British Blue.
Above left, Bicoloured longhair.
Left, Tabby shorthair.
Above right, British Blue.
Right and overleaf, Bicoloured longhairs.

Hunting and feeding

Although today the pet family cat is fed mainly from tins of prepared food and its meals are usually regular and sufficient, almost every adult cat, given the opportunity, will go out hunting into the garden or fields. The wild hunting instinct is very deeply rooted. The cat is a carnivore and in urban areas will take mainly mice, rats and birds, but in the country districts it will also hunt rabbits, hares, frogs, fish and even snakes.

The cat is a solitary, nocturnal hunter by nature, using mainly sight and sound to stalk its prey. When first alerted to the presence of a mouse at some distance away the cat crouches and then starts to stalk it with body flat to the ground. It then pauses crouched low with whiskers spread and ears turned forward. Stalking continues until the cat reaches the last available cover. The final attack is a short run, flat to the ground, followed by a pounce which is a thrust rather than a jump

Left, White longhair and black shorthair.
Right, Tabby longhair.
Below, Tabby shorthair.
Below right, White shorthair.

with the hind feet remaining firmly on the ground while the forepaws pin the mouse down with extended claws. The cat then finishes off its catch with a bite on the neck.

Even if a pampered town cat has no opportunity to go hunting the very same stalking actions will be seen as it chases a cotton reel or ball of wool.

A cat is a good climber and will readily climb trees in pursuit of a bird or to avoid a pursuing dog. It uses its claws for climbing. These are retractile and sheathed when not in use. They are kept in good condition by scratching with them on a tree trunk, which is a kind of honing. It is wise to provide your pet cat with a scratching-post if you wish to preserve your furniture!

Although a cat is not naturally at home in water, in some parts of the world cats enter water to catch fish. It is more usual, however, for them to sit on the bank of a stream and hook the fish out with the claws.

Left, Marmalade shorthair.
Right, Brown Burmese.
Below, Black shorthair.
Below right, Tabby shorthair.
Overleaf: Top left and bottom left, Marmalade shorthair.
Bottom right, Bicoloured longhair.
Right, Tabby longhair.

Play

One fact readily emerges from watching kittens playing: that the pattern is constant, leaving no doubt that it is innate or instinctive. Some of it may be varied by learning but mainly the pattern is the same. However much the kittens are enjoying their games, the play is a preparation for the more serious activities of adult life. In the wild a kitten has to learn to hunt for its food and all the movements of stalking prey are seen in its play with its littermates. The play consists of one kitten stalking another on flattened belly with tail lashing, leaping into the air as if clawing at a flying object, throwing small objects into the air and pouncing on them as they fall and chasing or stalking a ball or cotton reel. All these movements will later be used in hunting prey.

A mother cat will join in her kittens' play and encourage them to pounce on her tail and jump all over her. So, when she brings in a living mouse for the first time the kittens will naturally chase after it and instinctively use the neck bite to try and kill it.

Left and right, Marmalade shorthairs. *Below,* Marmalade shorthairs and tabby shorthair.

Communication

The cat has a definite language of its own communicated vocally and by gesture. The most familiar sound of all domestic cats is the *miaou*. It seems to be used most in communication with a human being, and not so much among cats themselves. It has infinite variations– it can tell you your cat is hungry or wants to be let out. It will vary when your cat is excited or displeased.

The most discordant sound made by a cat is the all too familiar 'yowling' which, especially at night, is so distressing. It is, however, only the voice of the male, or tom, seeking to impress the female. One of the most expressive sounds a cat makes is the hiss. Sometimes accompanied by a low growl the

Left, Tabby longhair.
Right, Blue-point Persian and Blue-point Himalayan or Colourpoint kittens.
Below, White Persian kittens.

hiss means the cat is very angry and is preparing for battle. When heard, it is better to get out of the cat's way.

Everybody knows the cat's purr of contentment and pleasure. Recent studies have shown that purring is produced by the vocal cords, the muscles of the larynx contracting rhythmically to produce a throbbing, resonant sound, with possibly the diaphragm acting as resonator.

Apart from vocalisations a cat will communicate by gesture—of its tail, its eyes, its ears or its whiskers. All cats have their own individual gestures but there are some common to all. Movement of the tail will express many moods; contentment, anger or concentration. A cat's face can show pleasure or pain especially by the expression of the eyes. The whiskers too can twitch with excitement or be laid back in fright. The arched back is a sign to its enemies that it will fight if necessary. Finally, the ears laid flat sideways indicate anger.

Left, Black shorthair.
Right, Marmalade shorthair.
Below, Bicoloured longhair.

Courtship and family life

Domestic cats are sexually mature at about 10 months. The height of the breeding season is from late December to March but the female may come on heat at intervals of 3-9 days from December to August. In warm countries or warm domestic conditions she may be receptive all the year round. She is at her best for breeding purposes from 2-8 years old and the male from 3-8 years. So often these days domestic cats are 'neutered' for the convenience of the household that normal courtship and family life are no longer so familiar.

Left, British Blue.
Right, Tabby longhair.
Below, Black shorthair.
Overleaf, Marmalade shorthair kittens.

If courtship and mating are allowed naturally, the tom is attracted by the smell of a female on heat. Several males will assemble and the courting of the female is accompanied by fighting amongst the toms and by the familiar 'yowling'. There is more noise then damage done, except perhaps an occasional torn ear or shoulder.

At first the female does not allow the triumphant male to approach her but he will continue to approach with a low call and without any aggression until gradually the female allows him to come close enough to touch her when he at once grips her by the back of the neck. If she is fully receptive mating then takes place.

If the mating is successful the kittens will be born after a gestation of about 65 days. The average litter size over all breeds is four kittens, but up to 13 is known. In the wild a cat will choose a dark, quiet place to have her kittens and as far as possible these conditions should be chosen for your domestic pet's confinement.

Left, Blue Persian and Odd-eyed White Persian kittens.
Right and below, Bicoloured shorthair cat and kittens.

After the birth of each kitten, the mother cleans off the birth membranes, bites through the umbilical cord, licks the kitten clean and eats the placenta (afterbirth). This extra food gives her nourishment for suckling her kittens. The kittens are born blind, deaf and only slightly furred.

The mother stays with her kittens almost continuously for the first few days feeding them and keeping them warm. A cat is a wonderful mother and if she feels there is any danger she will pick up her kittens by the scruff of the neck and transport each in turn to a safer place.

The kittens' eyes open between 4-10 days. By example, the mother will show her kittens how to wash themselves and how to play and hunt. By 2 months they are weaned and can feed themselves and when the mother starts to come into heat again they will be fully independent.

Left, Seal-point Himalayan or Colourpoint.
Right and below, Seal-point Siamese kittens.
Overleaf: Top left, White Persian kittens.
Bottom left, Blue, tabby and cream longhair kittens.
Right, Blue-point Himalayan or Colourpoint.

Intelligence

There are some scientists who would deny quite categorically that an animal, other than a human, could possess intelligence. They will tell you that all its actions are based on instinct and follow a fixed action pattern inherited through its genes. Most cat owners will heartily disagree with this point of view and insist that their particular pet shows great intelligence.

The trouble is to know how to define 'intelligence' when applied to a cat or other mammal and how to separate it from instinctive or insight behaviour. Instinctive behaviour is little better than automatic reflex action. When a cat is hungry it seeks food either by going to its food bowl or going into the garden to hunt a mouse. It requires little or no thought. Insight behaviour is the reaction to a new situation when the cat 'makes up its mind' in a flash as to what to do. Intelligence, on the other hand, has been defined as the ability to recognise a problem, formulate a solution and quickly act upon it. Could it not be called intelligence when my cat, that sleeps in a box in the kitchen, pushes the box over on its side on a

Left, Black shorthair.
Right and below, Tabby shorthairs.

very cold night so that he is protected from any draughts. He has found a solution to a problem. Probably a cat, being always sensitive to its own comfort, applies its intelligence more to any matter which affects its well-being!

Dogs have always been thought intelligent because they are trainable, obedient and able to learn simple tricks. Cats on the other hand are far too independent to learn tricks but that does not mean they are unintelligent. It may even mean that they are more intelligent because they still have the ability to look after themselves and lead the sort of life they want to rather than what their owner wants.

It may be that a cat or dog brought up in daily contact with a human being absorbs some of that person's intelligence and ability, just as a child brought up in an affluent and intellectual home seems to absorb knowledge and skills effortlessly from its environment. Maybe this intelligence is present also in truly wild animals but is latent, waiting only to be aroused by some unnatural or out-of-the-ordinary situation.

Left and right, Bicoloured longhairs.
Below, Cream longhair kittens.
Overleaf: Left, Marmalade shorthair.
Near right, top, Chinchilla.
Far right, top, Cream longhair.
Bottom right, Tabby and marmalade shorthairs.

Some popular breeds

There are many delightful colour photographs in this book showing some of the many popular breeds of cats, but there is only room here to describe a few. As has been said, there are basically two groups: long-haired and short-haired. All the long-haired cats conform to a general standard of having large, short, low-set bodies with short solid legs and of course a long, soft, silky coat, with long hair around the neck known as the frill. The tail is short, broad and bushy.

Left, White longhair.
Below, Black Persians.
Right, Bicoloured longhair and marmalade shorthair.
Far right, Tabby longhair.
Below right, Tabby shorthair.

The White Long-hairs or Persians
have been known in Europe for many
years. It is said the Angoras arrived first
from Turkey and then the Persians
came and the mating of these two types
produced the modern White Persians
or White Long-hairs. All are dignified,
beautiful cats, sensible of their long
tradition and even when playing do so
with grace and majesty. One of the oldest
Long-hairs is the rare Black. It has a jet
black coat and if perfect should have not
a single white hair. The most popular of
all Long-hairs in both Europe and
America is the Blue. A pure bred Blue
should have an even 'blue' colour all
over with no markings or white hairs.
It is quite a large cat but the enormous
frill round its neck makes it look even
larger. A truly handsome cat, the Blue is

Left, Cream longhair.
Right, Tabby shorthair.
Below, Marmalade shorthair.

quiet and affectionate. There are many other popular Long-hairs and many crosses from true breeds producing different colours and coats. Although the Long-hairs are beautiful cats their coats need daily brushing and combing as an addition to the cat's own natural grooming.

The short-haired group can be divided into those known as British (or Domestic in America), Foreign or Oriental and the Manx. The British Short-hairs have a powerful, stocky body with a round head and a short nose and broad muzzle. The legs are strong and sturdy and the fine coat is short and close. In this group is the Brown Tabby Short-hair, the traditional domestic cat with a friendly nature and the familiar 'tabby' colour and markings. The Black Short-hair is a large cat up to 14 lb in weight and if flawless should have not one white hair or any trace of brown in its coat.

The Foreign or Oriental breeds are those that have sleek coats, slim bodies and slanting eyes. Even if not imported they have an 'Oriental' look. One of the most popular cats today is the Siamese with its graceful, noisy, independent ways. Most Siamese are excellent hunters and although lovable always have something secretive in their look. There are a number of varieties. The Seal-pointed Siamese is perhaps the most popular with a pale cream coat shading to a deeper fawn towards the back. The points are deep brown, nearly black. The slanting eyes are a bright, clear blue. The kittens are particularly delightful.

Another beautiful, typically foreign-looking cat is the Abyssinian probably the nearest to the cats of Ancient Egypt. It has an intelligent, affectionate nature but is not so popular as the Siamese.

Finally there are the Manx cats with variously coloured coats and eyes, quite unlike any other cat in being tailless. They are popularly supposed to be a breed peculiar to the Isle of Man, but probably they were originally developed in Japan. Manx cats have a short back and deep flanks giving them a 'square' look. They are excellent hunters and skilled climbers.

Top left, White longhair.
Left, Seal-point Siamese.
Right, Tabby longhair.

Feral cats

The readiness with which a domestic cat goes back 'into the wild' or becomes feral shows how little in many ways it has changed from its wild ancestor, in spite of years of living with man. Many domestic cats take themselves off into the woods of their own accord but many unwanted cats are taken out into the countryside and abandoned. Most seem to survive and fend quite easily for themselves. Such cats seem to grow larger than usual, probably the result of a more active life and the abundance of natural food. One cat that went wild was reported to have doubled its size in 4

Left and right, Marmalade shorthairs.
Below, White and black shorthairs.

years. The maximum recorded length is 42 inches overall but it has been suggested that some may attain the maximum dimensions for the wild cat of 45 inches and 30 lb weight.

The number of feral cats in Britain alone must be very high but the number can only be surmised as a feral cat, in addition to its nocturnal habits, is wary of humans and if one is glimpsed in the woods it is difficult to know if it is really feral or only a domestic cat out on a hunting expedition.

Stories of unusual cats

Some years ago I was told the story of a pair of young rabbits caught and brought in by a cat, and fostered by her from an early age. As they grew up, they remained constant companions with the cat, and although they had the free run of the garden, never once did they

Left, Tabby longhair.
Right, British Blue.
Below, Tortoiseshell and white longhair.

attempt to burrow. This is just one of many freak-companionship stories.

A couple living in South Africa in 1954 had a she-cat that produced litters with monotonous regularity. The husband laid it down that from any future litter only one kitten should be kept. Several litters followed and accordingly all but one kitten from each was put to sleep. Then came the time when the cat produced a litter of one kitten only. "Clever girl" exclaimed the husband. Six weeks later mysterious noises were heard in the attic. Investigation revealed five more, well-fed kittens of the same age as the one downstairs!

The cat's dread of fire has sometimes been a factor in saving lives. Many years ago in Brighton, England, a cat awakened its mistress by loudly scratching at her bedroom door. The lady at first took no notice, but the cat was so persistent that at last she got out of bed and opened the door. Immediately the cat

Left, below and right, White longhair kittens.

gave her a knowing look and turned and walked down to the kitchen. Following the cat, the lady found the kitchen table and floor in flames, which had to be put out by the local fire brigade.

A young woman was aroused at night by her mother's cat scratching at her head. She pushed the animal away but it kept on pawing at her until she was obliged to rise. She found her mother, the cat's mistress, lying dead at the foot of the stairs. The older woman, who had remained downstairs after her daughter, had tried to climb the stairs and fallen and died.

Finally, a not unusual story of a well-loved cat I had in my old home. We were going on holiday the next day and Snooky was fetched to go to the cat kennels, some ten miles away. She was taken in a closed basket and we got ready to go away. The next morning early when I went downstairs there was Snooky sitting on the windowsill mewing to come in for his breakfast.

Left, Marmalade shorthair.
Below, Bicoloured shorthair.
Right, Tabby longhair.

The family cat

The information in this book has been mainly about the domestic cat's way of life and little has been said about its relations with its human owner. Although admittedly independent most cats, especially if reared from a kitten, are affectionate and need human companionship. A kitten taken into one's home should be petted and given as much attention as possible for the first few days so that it gets to know its owner. Given adequate freedom it will soon know its way about the house and garden and will repay you by years of keeping away mice from your home.

A kitten growing to adulthood in a family home with children will become a most important and well-loved member of the family and probably live to a ripe old age. My present cat is 18 years old and as healthy and active as ever he was.

Left, Tortoiseshell and white shorthair.
Below, Turkish-type shorthair.
Right, Cream longhair.
Overleaf: Left, Odd-eyed white Persian.
Right, Tabby, marmalade and cream longhair kittens.

INDEX

Pedigree cats are identified by breed (e.g. Burmese). The remaining cats are divided into longhaired and shorthaired types and then indexed under their colour varieties.

British Blue	14, 15, 30 55
Burmese	21
Chinchilla	6, 45
Colourpoint *see* Himalayan	
Himalayan blue-point	27, 39
Himalayan seal-point	36
Longhair, bicoloured:	
black-and-white	14, 16, 22
blue-and-white	42, 47
marmalade-and-white	7, 15, 17, 29, 43
Longhair, blue	38
Longhair, cream	2–3, 38, 42, 45, 48, 61, 63
Longhair, marmalade	63
Longhair, tabby	19, 23, 26, 31, 38, 47, 51, 54, 59, 63
Longhair, tortoiseshell-and-white	55
Longhair, white	4, 8, 18, 46, 50, 56, 57
Persian, black	46
Persian, blue	34
Persian, blue-cream	27
Persian, odd-eyed white	34, 62
Persian, white	27, 38
Shorthair, bicoloured	35, 58
Shorthair, black	8, 18, 21, 28, 31, 40, 52
Shorthair, marmalade	20, 22, 24, 25, 29, 32, 33, 44, 45, 47, 49, 52, 53, 58
Shorthair, Siamese-type	4
Shorthair, tabby	9, 14, 19, 21, 25, 41, 47, 49
Shorthair, tortoiseshell-and-white	60
Shorthair, Turkish-type	60
Shorthair, white	19, 52
Siamese, blue-point	11, 12
Siamese, lynx or tabby-point	12
Siamese, seal-point	10, 11, 13, 37, 50

Photographs supplied by:
Colour Library International Ltd., 80-82 Coombe Road, New Malden, Surrey, England.
and
Bruce Coleman Ltd., 16a-17a Windsor Street, Uxbridge, Middlesex, England.